FLY, GIRL, FLY!

SHAESTA WAIZ SOARS AROUND THE WORLD

BY
NANCY ROE PIMM
ILLUSTRATED BY
ALEXANDRA BYE

beaming books
MINNEAPOLIS

For my daughters—Ali, Lindsay, and Carli—wonderful examples of women of strength, tenderness, courage, and compassion. I love you all. —N.R.P.

To my parents—for believing me and encouraging my dream to be an artist. —A.B.

Hardcover ISBN: 978-1-5064-6468-8
Ebook ISBN: 978-1-5064-6665-1

Library of Congress Cataloging-in-Publication Data
Names: Pimm, Nancy Roe, author. | Bye, Alexandra, illustrator.
Title: Fly, girl, fly! : Shaesta Waiz soars around the world / by Nancy Roe
   Pimm : illustrated by Alexandra Bye.
Description: Minneapolis : Beaming Books, 2020. | Audience: Ages 5-8 |
   Summary: "The story of how Shaesta Waiz became the youngest woman in
   history, and the first woman from Afghanistan, to fly around the world
   in a single-engine aircraft"-- Provided by publisher.
Identifiers: LCCN 2019056259 (print) | LCCN 2019056260 (ebook) | ISBN
   9781506464688 (hardcover) | ISBN 9781506466651 (ebook)
Subjects: LCSH: Waiz, Shaesta, 1987---Juvenile literature. | Women air
   pilots--United States--Biography--Juvenile literature. | Air
   pilots--United States--Biography--Juvenile literature. | Afghan American
   women--Biography--Juvenile literature. | Flights around the
   world--Juvenile literature. | Aeronautics--Records--Juvenile literature.
Classification: LCC TL540.W247 P56 2020 (print) | LCC TL540.W247 (ebook)
   | DDC 629.13092 [B]--dc23
LC record available at https://lccn.loc.gov/2019056259
LC ebook record available at https://lccn.loc.gov/2019056260

VN0004589; 9781506464688; DEC2020

Beaming Books
510 Marquette Avenue
Minneapolis, MN 55402
Beamingbooks.com

In a big, big world was a small, small girl
who went by the name of Shaesta.

Born in a refugee camp in Afghanistan,
she did not remember when the soldiers came.

When the tanks rolled. When the bombs dropped.

She had no memory of her family's escape.
Or the plane ride to America.

In California, Shaesta's family grew and grew, until she was one of six girls. They chatted in Farsi and Pashto, the languages of their homeland. At dinnertime, they gathered around a cloth on the floor and ate, picnic style, from a spread of dishes.

At home, Shaesta lived as an Afghan, but in school she learned to be American.

One day, young Shaesta said, "I will do great things!"

Her mom said, "You can do anything you set your mind to!"

Her daddy patted her head and said,
"But *bachem*, my child, you are so shy."

Her sisters giggled.
"You are afraid of everything,
even planes in the sky!"

After she finished
high school, Shaesta's
cousins invited her
to Florida.

She would need to ride
in an airplane to get there.

Shaesta wondered,
Will it soar like a rocket or rumble like a roller coaster?
She boarded the aircraft and said a prayer.

The engines ROARED.

The wheels lifted.

And the
plane soared.

From up high, colors of brown, green, and gold flowed as one. No lines or borders separated one state from the next. Shaesta loved this view from above. A pilot's view.

One country. One big world. Up in the white, puffy clouds, Shaesta released her breath, along with her fears.

From then on,
Shaesta had one dream.
She told her family:

I want to be a pilot!

Many doubted Shaesta:

What Afghan man would
want to marry a woman
who flies?

Foolish dreamer.

Silly girl.

Girls do not belong in the cockpit of an airplane.

But Shaesta thought,
An airplane doesn't know if I'm a boy or a girl.

So she studied science and math. She read books. She applied for scholarships and took out loans to attend a school to learn how to fly. She became the first in her family to graduate college.

When she finally held her pilot's license, it felt like she had been granted a superpower. Shaesta wondered,
What now?

One day, Shaesta met Barrington Irving.
A Jamaican immigrant, Barrington grew up in poverty in Miami.
He had become the youngest man and first Black person
to fly solo around the world. Nothing had stopped him.

Shaesta started to dream about making her own solo flight around the world.

So she flew with Barrington over Russia and most of Asia to learn about international flying and radio calls.

Then she met Jerrie Mock, the first woman to fly solo
around the world. They talked about single-engine airplanes,
about big and little airports, about foreign countries,
about being alone, and about fear.

They talked about Amelia Earhart,
the first woman to fly across the Atlantic Ocean.
Amelia had said, "The most effective way
to do it, is to do it."

Shaesta decided she would not just fly all the way around the world. She'd also meet with young people everywhere. She'd get them excited about careers in science, technology, engineering, and math to chase down dreams of their own!

So Shaesta studied charts
and weather maps. She planned
and she plotted. She read letters
and emails from children all
around the globe who looked
forward to meeting her.

UNTIL . . .

Shaesta went wheels-up and set out
on her journey around the world.

At last, she soared!

As Shaesta flew across the Atlantic Ocean, she imagined the sharks, whales, and sea creatures swimming below. Shaesta shivered at the sight of icebergs poking through the ocean's surface.

Shaesta knew that so many things could go wrong on such a long flight.

If ice forms on my plane, it could become uncontrollable. I might fall from the sky!

Shaesta had never been so alone. There was not a boat in sight. No other planes in the sky. Not even a bird. Near the halfway point, the point of no return, she trembled.

Was this how Amelia Earhart had felt? And Jerrie Mock? Shaesta thought about giving up.

Instead, Shaesta took a deep breath and thought of the children. They expected to see her. Especially the girls from her homeland, Afghanistan.

Feeling the spirits
of Amelia and Jerrie
cheering her on,
Shaesta kept going.

She felt as big and powerful as the ocean below.

Country by country, Shaesta met with youth around the world. She told wide-eyed children her story and inspired them to follow their dreams. She landed in little-known places like Cagliari and Christmas Island. And faraway countries like Egypt and Fiji.

Some days, Shaesta soared through magical sunsets and topaz skies.

Other days, she battled sandstorms and dodged lightning strikes. Sometimes monsoons kept her tiny plane grounded for weeks. Many times she thought about quitting. But she pressed on.

When she reached Afghanistan,
Shaesta could not stop smiling.
Music played.
People cheered.
Women and girls hugged her—
and they wept.

They celebrated a girl with a dream, who dared to say that girls can soar and follow their hearts, wherever it may take them.

Months later, after flying nearly 25,000 nautical miles, with thirty stops on five continents, Shaesta landed at the airport where it all began. Shaesta Waiz had done it! She was the first woman from Afghanistan and, at thirty, was the youngest woman in history to fly a single-engine aircraft around the world.

Surrounded by family and friends, Shaesta kissed the ground. She was home.

AUTHOR'S NOTE

"YOU MUST BELIEVE IN YOURSELF AND ALLOW YOUR DREAMS TO SOAR."
—SHAESTA WAIZ

Every time Shaesta opened the door to an aircraft, she wondered how a woman like her could have a life like this. After all, she grew up a timid girl in a low-income area of California. As a refugee, she had trouble fitting in. Being an immigrant, English was her third language, and she read her first novel in tenth grade.

But when Shaesta found her love for aviation, she soared around the world to inspire the next generation. She wanted to be a living example to show that it is possible to achieve your dreams, regardless of the challenges you face.

As a graduate student at Embry-Riddle Aeronautical University in Daytona Beach, Florida, Shaesta knew the struggles female students faced following a male-dominated career path. In hopes of helping incoming students find success, she came up with an idea to create a team of "big sisters" to mentor and support young women studying aviation and engineering.

Over the years, the Women's Ambassador Program has met great success. Lou Seno, an engineering board member at the school, says, "Through the Women's Ambassador Program, Shaesta Waiz really helped raise the female enrollment at Embry-Riddle. Over the years, it has nearly doubled in size." As Shaesta prepared for her journey, she became the founder and president of Dreams Soar, a US-based global outreach nonprofit to promote science, technology, engineering, and mathematics (STEM). Through the organization, she planned to reach children in underserved communities and in regions unsupportive of women. Fifteen dedicated "dream team" members worked tirelessly to get Shaesta in the air so she could encourage youth, especially girls, to follow careers in aviation and STEM. Many sponsors supported the mission—big companies who believed in Shaesta's big dream. The companies that supported Shaesta wanted to bring awareness to the need for more women pilots. In 2017, only about 4 percent of the pilots in the United States and the United Kingdom were female. As of 2019, around 7 percent of pilots are women.

On her global flight, Shaesta visited refugee camps and orphanages. When she returned to Afghanistan, the land of her birth, Shaesta saw hope in the eyes of the many girls who had gathered to welcome her. In Afghanistan, some girls are prohibited from getting an education. According to a 2018 World Bank report, about 70 percent of women over age fifteen are unable to read. The president of Afghanistan, Ashraf Ghani, invited Shaesta to his palace. He promised her that her story would be told in future history books, acknowledging Shaesta as the first certified female pilot from Afghanistan, and he named her Afghanistan's Ambassador of Peace.

A MESSAGE FROM SHAESTA

As I went around the world by myself in a small airplane in 2017, I had the chance to meet with over three thousand girls and boys from twenty-two different countries. After talking with these incredible kids about the exciting careers that exist, I was reassured of how important it is to inspire the next generation.

One of the stops along the global flight was to my homeland in Kabul, Afghanistan. Going back home was so special for me. It had been almost thirty years since my family and I had to leave because of war. During my stop in Kabul, I met so many young girls who looked just like me. Few of them had big dreams to get an education and help rebuild Afghanistan. Unfortunately, some of the girls said they didn't think they were strong enough to make a difference, and others doubted they were smart enough to go to school.

This inspired a new dream to build a STEM school in Afghanistan. I hope this school will empower girls to get an education and contribute to their society by working on STEM-based projects that serve their communities. I have learned that every great achievement starts with a dream.

I hope this story inspires you to always believe in yourself and to soar forward with your dream, no matter how daring that dream may be.

SW